there's a Hole in My Sidewalk

the romance of self-discovery

portia Nelson

ATRIA BOOKS
New York London Toronto Sydney New Delhi

BEYOND WORDS
Hillsboro, Oregon

ATRIA BOOKS
A Division of Simon & Schuster, Inc.
1230 Avenue of the Americas
New York, NY 10020

BEYOND WORDS
20827 N.W. Cornell Road, Suite 500
Hillsboro, Oregon 97124-9808
503-531-8700 / 503-531-8773 fax
www.beyondword.com

Managing editor: Lindsay S. Brown
Design: Devon Smith

First Atria Books/Beyond Words hardcover edition February 2012

ATRIA BOOKS and colophon are trademarks of Simon & Schuster, Inc.
Beyond Words Publishing is a division of Simon & Schuster, Inc.

For more information about special discounts for bulk purchases, please contact Simon & Schuster
Special Sales at 1-866-506-1949 or business@simonandschuster.com.

The Simon & Schuster Speakers Bureau can bring authors to your live event.
For more information or to book an event, contact the Simon & Schuster Speakers
Bureau at 1-866-248-3049 or visit our website at www.simonspeakers.com.

Manufactured in the United States of America

10 9 8 7 6 5 4 3 2 1

The Library of Congress has cataloged the 1993 edition as follows:

Nelson, Portia.
  There's a hole in my sidewalk: the romance of self-discovery / by Portia Nelson.
        p.   cm.
Originally published: Los Angeles; Popular Library, 1977.
1. Self-realization. 2. Self-perception. 3. Maturation (Psychology). 1. Title.
BF637.S4N45 1993
158'.1—DC20

                                                                    93-18380

ISBN: 978-1-58270-377-0
ISBN: 978-1-4516-8635-7 (ebook)

The corporate mission of Beyond Words Publishing, Inc.: *Inspire to Integrity*

"I am part of all
that I have met."

—Tennyson

To all of you,
whoever you are,
I humbly dedicate this book.

PERSONAL NOTE

I choose to call these thoughts "pieces"... pieces of me. These pieces have had a bit of trouble finding a comfortable concept that would knit them into one book... just as I have had difficulty molding a multi-faceted misfit into one person.

More than anything, they are evidence, to me, that here in the middle of my life I have finally gained a small pin-point of self-awareness... false images stripped away... "through a glass darkly, but, now... face to face." No hiding, anymore, behind innocence and ignorance.

It isn't necessarily easier now... but I have a self that I trust and feelings and the experience are mine... not what I should feel... not what I was taught to feel and not something someone else felt that I admired and imitated. Knowing one's own feelings and being able to trust them is the difference between existing and living. So, that's what I have here, I guess... living and loving experiences... pieces of my small universe that can, I hope, be recognized by yours.

EDITOR'S NOTE

I am pleased to present the 35th Anniversary Edition of *There's a Hole in My Sidewalk*. This extraordinary book was originally published in 1977, and since then it has become a well-loved classic. The humor, inspiration, insight, and comfort found within these pages have touched thousands of people. *There's a Hole in My Sidewalk* is not just another book that sits on the shelf; it is a trusted friend people turn to time and again. I am thrilled to be reissuing a book that has offered so many people hope and inspiration.

The opening poem, "An Autobiography in Five Short Chapters," has been quoted in more than two hundred books. This simple, elegant poem depicts a universal journey that is at once deeply human and unwaveringly straightforward, and has helped guide many on their own path to self-discovery. If you are familiar with only this poem, I think you will be delighted to read the entire work.

Portia Nelson's writing is a clear, honest depiction of self-reflection, inner conflict, personal struggle, and, ultimately, resilience, personal growth, and hope, which has resonated deeply with those making transitions in their lives. *There's a Hole in My Sidewalk* has been especially significant to those recovering from addiction, as well as their loved ones, and has been used in many 12-step and recovery programs. As the publisher of this book, Beyond Words is honored to contribute to this tradition.

In the late 1990s, I had the pleasure of spending time with Portia Nelson in New York where she lived at the time. What a lovely woman she was! Portia led an accomplished life and left us with an impressive legacy that spans an acting career, which includes her role in the classic movie *The Sound of Music*, her body of work as a singer and composer, which includes five solo albums on major labels, and her work as writer, a result of which you now have in your hands. Although Portia is no longer with us, she is here in spirit, speaking to our hearts from the pages ahead.

I am proud to help continue Portia's legacy with this special edition. To celebrate this milestone we are releasing the book in hardcover for the first time, thus creating an enduring package to hold this timeless classic. I know that this book will continue to have great meaning in numerous lives for many more years to come. My hope is that one of those lives will be yours.

Cynthia Black
President and Editor in Chief
Beyond Words Publishing

CONTENTS

A story of
ME in You
and
You in Me
in
Five Short Chapters

PROLOGUE

My life has been a series
        of wonderful experiences.
It's a pity I wasn't there
        for most of them.

AUTOBIOGRAPHY IN FIVE SHORT CHAPTERS

Chapter One

I walk down the street.
>There is a deep hole in the sidewalk.
>I fall in.
>I am lost.... I am helpless.
>>It isn't my fault.
It takes forever to find a way out.

Chapter Two

I walk down the same street.
>There is a deep hole in the sidewalk.
>I pretend I don't see it.
>I fall in again.
I can't believe I am in this same place.
>>But, it isn't my fault.
It still takes a long time to get out.

Chapter Three

I walk down the same street.

> There is a deep hole in the sidewalk.
> I see it is there.
> I still fall in…it's a habit…but,
>> my eyes are open.
>> I know where I am.

It is *my* fault.

I get out immediately.

Chapter Four

I walk down the same street.

> There is a deep hole in the sidewalk.
> I walk around it.

Chapter Five

I walk down another street.

CHAPTER ONE

I don't know what I want sometimes,
But I know
that I want to know
what I want.
I know that once I know what I want
I will be able to get it.
Of course, I may not want what I get
when I get it....
But, at least
I'll know I don't want that!
Then, I can move on to something else
I don't know if I want.
That's progress!

You say you love me for who I am....
But...
who you think I am
            is not *who* I am.

Therefore,
it's hard for me to be who I am
            when we're together...

because...
I think I have to be
            who you think I am.

Of course,
I don't know exactly who it is
            you think I am...
I just know it isn't who I am.

Who am I?
Well...
Who I am is something I recognize
when someone tells me
who I am *not*.
At least, I *think* that's *not* who I am.
Maybe who I am *not*
            is who I *am*!
If that's who I am... MY GAWD...
            you really love me.

I used to suffer a great deal
thinking I was the only one
in the world
so lonely
and troubled.

Then, I opened the door to myself
and discovered there were
millions
of people
just like me.

It isn't lonely anymore…
but it's miserable to be
so ordinary.

I know why we are friends.
It's because I don't always
approve of you.

You don't think you deserve approval.
So… if I gave it to you,
you would not
approve of me
and I would lose your trust.

Friendship is based on trust
and I want you
to trust me
because I need your approval.

However, if I get your approval,
I will not trust you
because I don't think I deserve approval
either.

I know why we are friends.

You want to please me... and,

I want to please you...

>so please make the decision
>about where we are going tonight.

If I make the decision...
>and then *you* don't like it,
>you'll be mad at me
>and I'll be miserable all evening
>because I haven't pleased you.

Now... if *you* try to please me...
>and *you* make the decision,
>and I don't like it
>when we get there...
>at least *you* will be pleased.

If I am unhappy with where we are,
>or what we are doing,
>that alright...

because it won't be my decision
that will have made you unhappy.
>It will be yours.
>Therefore,
>it will be *your* fault!
>>*That* will please me.

You say you will never leave me
        because I understand you.
And I love being thought of
        as "understanding."

But, I also understand
        that by being so understanding,
        you automatically
        have the freedom
        to do as you please...
        because...
if I am not understanding,
        you will leave me.

I think that what I really
        have to understand is this:
In order to be so understanding all the time
        (so that you will not leave me),
        I have to leave myself.

If I am not myself
        when I am being so understanding,
        who the hell is it
        you will never leave?

Better I should not be so understanding
        so there's somebody
        you can leave.

You have made a fool of me!

I know that I am not the most beautiful,
the most talented, the most intelligent
        person in the world…
        but I liked you…
        and I wanted you
        to think I was.
So… I tried to be beautiful
        talented and intelligent
        for you.

However,
        since I succeeded
        in making you believe it,
naturally,
        I immediately
        lost respect for you
        for not seeing
        that I had fooled you.

Now…
        I am intelligent enough,
        beautiful enough and
        talented enough

not to be associated with fools…
and I am incensed that I didn't see
      how foolish you were
          at once.

But…
      I liked you then… and…
it drove me to make you believe
      what I wanted you to believe….

Except…
      I was so convincing,
      I began to believe it myself!

Now…
      anybody who believes
      things like that about me
         is a fool.

That makes me a fool!

And if it weren't for you
      believing what I wanted you to believe,
      I wouldn't know that.

I hate you for making a fool of me!

Will you please stop trying to
      finish my sentences before I do?

It's humiliating!

After all… it's my sentence!
      Let me show it off!

I know you are really trying to let me know
      how sensitive and smart you are…
      and how deeply you understand me….

But… if you are that smart…
      please let me think that
      I am smarter than you
      by not impressing me with
      how smart you are
      in the middle of my sentences!

Of course,

     if I am smart enough
     to be aware of
     what you are up to…

Then,

     I should be smart enough to know
     it doesn't matter what you do
     in the middle of my sentences.

Maybe I'm not so smart!

Now, that *is* humiliating!

I want you to love me…
> but I am aware
> that you only love
> what you cannot get.
> So, I can't let you know
> that I am interested
> or you won't love me back.

Now…
> I hate games
> and dishonesty
> more than anything.

Therefore…
> if I love you enough
> to be dishonest…
> to play a game
> in order to keep you interested,
>> I will hate myself.
> If I hate myself,
>> eventually,
>> I will crack up!

If I crack up...
    at least,
    you won't be able to get me...
        because I won't care...
        or be aware
        that you even exist...
    and then,
    maybe you will love me.

Jesus! There's got to be a simpler way!

You are strong… vital…
　　　very much in control of yourself.
I admire that!
I know you can help me…
　　　and I need help.

But,

　　　if I allow you to help me,
　　　I will have to trust you enough
　　　to give up my own self control.

If I give that up,
　　　I will begin to feel powerless…
　　　without identity…
　　　like a nobody!

How dare you help me to be a nobody!

I cannot seem to leave you…
  though often,
  I think I should because
  even though I care…
I am not in love with you.
But I am in love with the fact
  that you are in love with me.
It makes me think very well of myself,
When I think well of myself,
  I am very nice…
  and very creative.
That makes me feel worthwhile and then
  I love myself.
The more I love myself…
  the more you love me.
No wonder I can't leave.
  I wouldn't know
  I loved myself…
  without you.

I would like to be one…
A one not worried about being two!
I am more one
      when we are three.
When we are two,
      I become a zero.
I become zero because
I am afraid you will see
      that I am not one.
When we are three, I am comfortable…
It doesn't matter if I am not one
      since I seem to become one
      simply because
      there are two being two
      and letting me be one.
Therefore, I am not zero… I can't be…
Two from there is always one.
So, I am more one when we are three…
      as long as I don't worry about
            being two.

In the beginning
　　　everywhere I went,
　　　I didn't always go along.
I didn't know it then,
　　　but I was afraid I'd meet myself
When we finally met,
I wasn't who I expected I'd be…
　　　but, oh, it was a relief
　　　to have someone to be with…
　　　　　　　at last.

CHAPTER TWO

I am a hopeless romantic
        who does not believe
        love solves everything.
Still, I weep for the loss
            of illusion…
        knowing full well
           that reality
        is unbearable…
without a few gilded window frames
           to see through.

How brazen you are!

You lean across the table…
      slender hands
      cupping your face…

and stare arrow-straight
      into my eyes…
      no blinking at all.

You know you are making a frame

for a remarkably beautiful face.

I stare back…
      not out of desire
      or challenge…

      but as my only defense
      against your discovering

how deeply I am immersed in pleasure.

I hope that what you are after
is an exchange…
not
a reaction.

One step forward
        into the bright of loving.
Yet, I fear the bright will not last.
        …so, one step back.
Still, I fear more,
        the dark of not loving at all.
Well then…
        may I take a giant step?
        May I?
I have already answered.
        Shall we dance?

I know who you are.

You are so much of me
        that if I don't love you
        I won't exist.

And I'm selfish.
        I don't want to miss anything.

Two days ago
I never would have believed
I would spring from my bed
        at the first glimmer
                of sunlight…
and drive all over town
        looking for
        blue Volkswagens!

Dear one…

Kind one…

> lend me your dreams
> for a while.

Cover me
> with the sweet sleep
> of your innocence,
and wake me
> with the crystal sunshine
> of your hope.

Light my darkness with fireflies
> and build me air castles
> to house
> the velvet summers
> of love.

Stay with me,
> dear one…
stay with me long enough
> to let me hear again,
> that far away music
> of yesterday…
> > when I was young.

Your hair is like a monk's cap
          made of wheat.

It often slips down over your eyes
          so I can't see if you are
          hiding from me
          or spying on me.

Sometimes
          I reach out...
          as an artist might...
and make a gentle brush stroke
          on the canvas of your brow
          to change the shape of your cap.

As much as I love it,
I cannot bear to talk to you
          without watching your eyes.

Besides,
          there is such selfish pleasure
          in the act of touching,
          lightly...
          hardly at all...
making a graceful arc there
and seeing you smile...
          as if your hair were attached
          to the corners of your mouth.

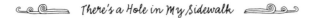

There is so much about me that I don't know
until I talk to you.

That first day…
　　　　　as you turned to leave…
　　　　　we touched…
and, like magnets, we clung to one another
　　　　　for a long time.
　　　　　Nothing more.
Yet…in that rare moment of holding you
I experienced what I have come to value most…
　　　　　the ecstasy
　　　　　of
　　　　　not doing anything
　　　　　about it.

How wise of you to wait…
to fill the shy, awkward spaces
     with white wine
     and cushioned conversation.
I am aware that you are
     allowing me time
     to become accustomed
to the cities of your smile…
and to window shop your eyes…
     until, at last,
     I am so full of you,
that I no longer blush
     on my way into your arms.

Water, Air, Earth, Fire.

Mix together slowly,
          with ceiling seagulls
          and pear wine.

Stir until the perfect blend...

Cool for a moment... then,
          place in the fruitful womb
          of love
          to be born again
          into a circle of light...

an enchanted world where only believers
          are allowed to enter.

I can feel my fear beginning
                    to settle inside me…
                    like sleepy kittens
                    upon the hearth
Shshshsh…tip toe…
Don't slam doors in my mind…
                    not now.
Let the kittens sleep a little while
                    please…
The fire will die soon enough, anyway…
And now, while the world is warm…
                    hold me.

I think I just fell into a hole
in the sidewalk.

I have said, "I love you"…
　　　before you,
　　　and meant it.

Yet,
I would have to admit…
　　　that laid on the scales,
　　　the pain of loving
　　　has often outweighed the joy.

But, it never ceases to amaze me
　　　that I never died of love.

Looking back…
　　　knowing I survived…
　　　pain has become my faith.

Though I am fragile…
　　　it is my strength.

So, I warn you…
　　　I will not die of you.

I know that pain and joy
        cannot be separated…
        and, like tomorrow and today
        they become one another.

And so, I remember those
        before you,
and rejoice that I said,
        "I love you"
        before you…

because,
it will help me not to die of you…
        like I didn't
        before you.

I am always a grumbling sleepwalker
in the mornings.

Do you realize…
for three days in a row
I have laughed
at least ten times
before coffee?

It's a dreary day....
Let's just stay inside.
We can pretend that
        Kisses are brushes
        and that we are
        each other's canvases.
We won't need a northern light...
        or any light at all,
        for that matter....
And who cares if we ever finish
        the picture, anyway.

Sorry I didn't answer.
I was listening
       to what you weren't saying.

Portia Nelson

You are the oldest young person
            I have ever known.
It makes me feel younger than you are.
            That's a neat trick!

I am so free with you,
I never wish to be
free of you.

The beautiful togetherness
                    of our silence
                    makes me wonder
why we ever bothered
                    to speak at all.

I didn't really
leave my heart
in San Francisco…
although I said I did….
But, I certainly
let it out
into the fresh
morning air
and ran it up and down
a few hills.
I did let it rest
in the smile
of a beautiful stranger
for a few days…
But then,
I snatched it away
and brought it home
to you…
as I knew I would
before I went away
to be mad at you.

I think I love you most
    in those early hours
    just before sunrise
When,
    spent with loving
    and lost in dreaming,
You reach out,
    like the morning glory vine,
    and wind about,
    braiding limb to limb,
        binding me to you
        with the tender quiet
        of us.
Desire is buried in slumber…
and,
    asking nothing…
    giving all…
You bend to touch me
    through a thousand years of knowing
    …without knowing.
But I know.
I'm glad I'm a light sleeper.

When I listen
to your feelings,
and can feel
your listenings…
Only then
can I expect you
to hear me.

We are not "in love"…
but, we are love.
I'm glad.
It lasts longer.

My longing is burning a hole
      in my patience....
        Time is spinning away.
What good is sleep
      when an eternity
      is rushing by
      that I could be kissing you?

Damn it!
Will you please wake up?
I think I'll turn over...
      a little bump
      never hurt anybody!
"Hey!... awake so early?
      I love you."

Please understand…
There are days I must leave you…
            in order to be closer to you.
Up close, I cannot search out
            those fragments of you
            that your image of yourself
            hides from me.
At a distance…
            uncluttered be sensation…
            I can really see you, freely…
            and discover pieces of myself,
                  as well.
And then, we come home together…
            to love you all the more.

You said you didn't love me
                this morning.
I didn't believe you.
I knew you just hated yourself.
                That's alright.
I don't love you either…
                today.

Please…
don't extract promises from me
that must race quickly
      from the present
      into the past
casting dark shadows on the future.
Now… today… is all
      we can be certain of
      and love
      is something better
than a collection of pretty vows
to cling to on a rainy day.
What we already are
      is what we will be
         together.
      Isn't that enough?

Stop looking at me like that!
Can't you see how much
          I need you to believe
          what I am saying
so that I can believe it
          myself?

I would give you everything…
                    if I could…but,
the only gift worth giving
                    is freedom…
the freedom to grow…
                    away from me
                    if necessary.
Of course, one can't give freedom,
but, at least I know that.
Maybe that's the gift then…
                    the knowing….
And I couldn't tie a ribbon around it
                    even if I wanted to.

Ask something of me…
            please.
I know there is no answer…
            but often,
I need to feel it would be me
            you would ask…
if there was one.

I am not locking out!
I am trying very hard
        not to lock you in!
Maybe it's, the same thing

What you seek is my approval…
       not my self.
So, it is more friendly
       that I turn you
       back to your self…
       the source
       of acceptance.
When you no longer need
       my approval…
I can give it to you.

You say you love me
           because I understand you
           better than you understand
                    yourself.

Sometimes, like now,
           I wish I didn't
           because it forces me to see
           that it is also the reason
           you will have to
                  leave me.

You slept on your own side of the bed
                last night….
It was a universe wide.
When I reached out to touch you
                all I could feel
                was the distance
                between.
It is still there today.
Your eyes… that soft bed blue…
                once my resting place…
are crowded with distant mountains
                and racing rivers.
And I'll be alone…
                with you…
                again tonight.

This is no carnival!
     I can ride with you…
     but,
     I am not
     your
     merry-go-round.
When you have discovered
     the difference…
I'll meet you at the Ferris wheel.

I don't smoke…

    so…

I never thought
    I would miss the stale smell
    of your bent,
    charred cigarretes
    on my bedside table.

    But,

    the clean ashtray
    was as glaring
    as a headlight,
    last night.

    I couldn't sleep.

If I smoked…

    maybe I wouldn't have noticed
    you were gone.

    Maybe.

Let me be angry…
    please.
    It is the only way
I can keep you from seeing
    how much
    I need you.

If I say "no" to you
                I will lose you.
If I say "yes"…
                I will lose myself.
Even if I win, I lose.
                Or do I?

I am not a piece of jewelry
       to be worn
       so that others will admire you.
If you choose to continue…
       you must also remember
       that when jewelry is displayed
       … it can be stolen.

Will you try… just once,
          to be my age?
I'm tired of
          trying to be yours.

Stand up.
Let go of my hand.
Maybe then…
          I can let go of yours.
          You first.

I know you heard me…
     but were you listening?

Better stop now,
  before smiles become tightropes
  for words that step...
  with measured coolness...
across mechanical lips into deaf ear.

Please get the hell out of my life…
      only…
      go softly…
      and don't let me see you go…
or I may call you back…
      and there is no one home.

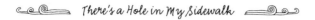

Wait!
You can't leave me now.
What will I do with all these
Oreo cookies?

I warn you... I will not die of you.

I warn you... I will not die of you.

The silence is so loud,
I cannot hear my own advice.

Love, love… where are you?
You alone soothe the ache…
     and I cannot believe in you.

Today…
I know how lonely I am
        for you.
I have mistakenly called
        four people
        by your name.

The most I can hope for,
        right now,
is to make it to tomorrow…
        just once…
without listening
        for the phone.

I made the bed today.
I almost thought I was over you
       … for a minute.

I never lied to you.
I always told you the truth
about love.

The joke is:
You listened to me.
I didn't.

CHAPTER THREE

I crowed
What I knowed
Bestowed
What I knowed
You hoed
What I knowed
And growed
What I knowed
But I slowed
What I knowed
And stowed
What I knowed
Then you goed
Up the road
And I blowed
What I knowed.

I know myself…
Now that you have left…
        I shall be everywhere
        hoping to make such memories
                with someone else.
That is when I will really feel
                you have gone.

My body is suspended…
My mind is lost in space…
My tongue just wobbles loosely
                back and forth…
Saying nothing…
Doing nothing…
Out of time and out of place.
Like a bird…in dead of winter…
                flying north.

What were you…?
Who were you…?
Something in me… I know that.
       But you were like a drug.
While you were near,
       you were the ultimate "high."
With you… I could split atoms,
       stop time…
       stay young…
Or I thought I could.
But you only gave out small doses of yourself,
       enough to keep me coming back.
And I could never be sure
       when you would be available again.
Soooo… the inevitable crash… withdrawal!
I won't break windows, kill,
       or steal for a "fix"…
but I sometimes feel I might die
       for need of you.

As with tennis…
        never play "Love"
        with someone
        whose game
is not as good as yours.
You'll end up losing…
        and they won't
        know enough
        to care.

Without ever having you…
        I have lost you.
Without ever knowing you…
        I know you…
There is no history…
        Only a memory
        that never occurred at all.
        A memory…
        I can never forget.

It was a certain kind of sun, then…
And dreams and hopes hung like thick smoke
                              in the air.
Lyrics of songs jumped out at me
                    like playful kittens around
                                      a corner.
It is a long-remembered, half-forgotten time.
Where is it now?
Waiting for me… or for you… somewhere?
Or has it gone its way…
                    like the morning of your smile?

We weren't living together,

anyway.

We were hiding together.

"Pain and loneliness make you strong…"
I dish that one out a lot!
Today, I don't want to be strong.
I want to dream just as much
as anybody else.
But, I keep on paying my dues, anyway,
and I really don't want
to belong
to that club
anymore.

You were so busy finding yourself
in me…
That I had to run from you
To keep you from killing
both of us.

Have you learned yet,
That who you know
          is not
          who you are?

The softer I walk
The louder I hear.

To own anything
   is to be owned by it.
I never wanted to own you....
   It's impossible....
And I never wanted to be owned.
But, I guess
   I always wanted you
   to pretend
   that you thought
   I was worth owning.

If all the "ifs" and "maybes,"
"wish-I-weres" and
        "could-have-beens-
        if-only-things-
        were-different-
        than-they-are"
could fall right off a cliff…
maybe I'd discover how
        to live with
        what is here and now…
but then,
I might as well forget this
        'cause I started it
                with "if."

In those moments of despair…
when I really don't care
whether or not I survive,
then, am I most keenly aware
of the certainty that I will.
That's the pain of it…
and the miracle.

CHAPTER FOUR

I am astounded
    at how long it takes
        to discover…
    for the first time,
the things I have learned…
    over and over again
      all my life.

The real growth
        is in recognizing
        that we do
        always get
what we want in life…
        one way or another.

Nobody's perfect!
    Somebody doesn't have to be.

Most loneliness
        is pain…
peering into mirrors
        of self-pity
        with the hope
        of seeing someone else
          to blame it on.

Listen to what you criticize
                most severely
And you will hear
                what you most fear
                you are.

I was always afraid of
                risking *risk*.
But I found that I could stand
                to risk *risk*
better than I could stand
                to fear *fear*.
At least, risking
                brought about changes…
and the changes took up so much time,
I forgot what it was I was afraid
                to risk losing…
                in the first place.

The nicest thing about my life, now, is
that I am here with me
most of the time.

There is no such thing
       as perfect freedom…
There is only the freedom to
       discover
       that there is
no such thing
       as perfect freedom!

It is much easier to be lonely
without someone…
than it is to be lonely
with someone.

Real belief
   is a quiet thing…
   too busy being itself
   to look for disciples.

It is a waste of time and energy
to worry about
what others are thinking
about you.

because…

You can never know
exactly what another person
is thinking…AND,
the worst part it…
they are usually not thinking
about you at all.

They are too busy worrying about
what others
are thinking about them.

So, the truth is, all those terrible thoughts
you thought they might
be thinking about you,
are your own thoughts
about yourself.

Better spend your energy
        worrying about that…or,
                you just might
                convince somebody to think
what you were afraid
        they might be thinking
                        after all.

It isn't always best
          to let everything
          spill out.
At times,
          there is more to be gained
          by using restraint!
Remember,
          it is the water
          held back by the dam
          that lights the city!

Always trying
         to be a good person
can be the biggest block
         to becoming one.

To live happily with a pet,
one must first accept
      the responsibility
      of disciplining it
      consistently and firmly
      with much love!
To live happily with ourselves…
      it is the same.

Who you are
　　　is not
　　　who you were…
It is who you are.

Any day of the week
I would choose to be "out"
      with others
      and in touch
      with myself…
than to be "in" with others
      and out of touch
      with myself.

I can tell how secure I am now.
I no longer clean the house
        the day before the maid comes!

Love is not a thing
to be "in" or "out" of.
It just is.
The beginning is the ending…
and the ending… the beginning…
Always and
never…
forever.

In youth…
            man seems to satisfy loneliness
                        with passion….
And in maturity…
            aloneness…with compassion.
What a pity the difference
            is most often discovered
            after muscle and bone
            can no longer climb
                        to the top
                        of the mountain.

I have come to regard unrequited love
like a hole in a sock.
Mend it, or discard it!
Don't just stand there with cold feet!

Disciplining one's self
    can be carried
    too far.
It is alright to relax
    part of the time.
Even the soils is richer
    when it rests
    every seven years.

If I keep talking about
what I believe in…
Eventually…
I will tell myself
how much I believe in
what I talk about.

Since I've finally
    taken responsibility
    for my life—
I can't tell you how often
    I've wanted
    to give it back.

    But, nobody wants it.

    Isn't that lucky?

Nothing matters, now.
I mean…

  everything matters so much
that nothing matters now.

Alone can be beautiful.
It's the one truth
     we know to be certain.
     We are
     A Lone.
To embrace that truth
     is the first step
     to becoming
     Al One!

CHAPTER FIVE

I walk down another street.

Aware and alive
to the little I know,
as if I've arrived
at another plateau.
A plateau…familiar…
yet,
wonderfully strange
where I find my milieu
in the fortunes of change.

In my soul is a room
with a wedding inside….
Alone
is the groom
and Truth is
the bride.

Pity has gone
    to its place on a shelf…
    to be summoned for others
    but
    rarely for self.
        Touching and feeling
        in heart and in brain
        Accepting the healing
        of joy
        that's in pain….

Where *Alone* is not gloom,
    nor a fearsome divide.
        Alone is the groom
        and the Truth is
        the bride.

Your alone-ness
　　　　nourishes and protects
　　　　　　my own.
I am always on the watch
　　　　　　for you.
No need to wear a carnation!
I'll know you… by me…
　　　　　　but you can hurry
　　　　　　if you want to.

EPILOGUE

I know you, by me…
and me, by you.
A mirrored exchange
of awareness…loving.
Loving awareness…
Always becoming…
becoming always
more you in me
and me in you…
Growing separately together…
changing and remaining the same,
eternally.

ABOUT THE AUTHOR

Portia Nelson was a renaissance woman: author, singer, actress, composer, lyricist, painter, and photographer. She has appeared in such films as *The Sound of Music*, *Dr. Doolittle*, *The Trouble with Angels*, and *The Other*, as well as on the television soap opera *All My Children*, as Mrs. Gurney for many years. She performed on Broadway in the award-winning musical *The Golden Apple*.

Over the years she has written the music and lyrics for many revues, television specials and films. Her song "Make a Rainbow" was sung by Marilyn Horne at President Clinton's inaugural ceremony.

As a singer, Ms. Nelson recorded five show albums for Columbia Records and three additional solo albums. She was also included in the Smithsonian collections *Cole Porter Songs* and *The American Popular Song*.

There's a Hole in My Sidewalk was made into a musical based on the book, and played at the York Theatre in Manhattan. Portia directed, wrote both the music and lyrics, and performed in the production.

There's a Hole in My Sidewalk was originally published in 1977 by Popular Library and was reprinted by the author in 1988. Since that time, the book has become a sought-after classic, but very hard to find. The poem "Autobiography in Five Short Chapters" has been reprinted in numerous publications. If you wish to use any of the material in this book, please contact the publisher.